Purpose At The Park

A Simple Four-Step
Community Outreach Guide by
Pastor Steve Baney, M. Div.

Published in Ashland, Ohio, USA
In 2012
By Steve Baney, M. Div.

Printed in the United States of America
by Lulu.com

ISBN 978-1-105-84424-9

Scripture designated NIV is quoted from
Holy Bible, New International Version.
Wheaton: Tyndale House, 1988.

Scripture designated NLT is quoted from
Holy Bible, New Living Translation.
Wheaton: Tyndale House, 1997.

Purpose at the Park is a special outreach designed to connect the local congregation with the local community. Each Sunday night at 7:00 pm between June 10 and July 29, the City Park will host live music at Needle Hall stage. Group members will get to enjoy the live music while following a simple plan to reach out to people who are within our community but are not yet a part of our congregation. The plan involves a 4-step process, based on the word PARK.

P - **Pray** for the people around you. Arrive early (music starts at 7) to pray for the people who will sit near you. Ask God to place someone near you who needs to experience the love and grace of Christ.

A - **Ask** them something. When a person sits down near you, tell them your name and ask for their name. Ask about their kids. Ask about their dog, or ask anything that will start a conversation. If the person seems interested in conversation, then...

R - **Recruit** them to attend worship. We'll provide a number of tools you can use to invite people to worship, specific things you can say or do to make this process of invitation easier.

K - **Keep on**. Keep on praying. Keep on building a relationship with them. If you see them next week, keep on sitting by them. It may take all summer of friendly conversation before a person is ready to be invited and come to worship.

How to use this book

You'll want to read the whole introduction now. Then read each weekly section as you progress through the summer. These instructions are designed to be flexible for your schedule. If you miss a week, don't skip the section. Go through the material at your own pace. Keep track of your progress by writing the date in the space provided.

Before you go to the park each week, read through the next section of the material. It will give you some Scripture to read, some key points to reflect upon, and specific steps to take when you are at the park.

Memorize the words from the acronym for PARK (Pray, Ask, Recruit, and Keep On). This will be your basic pattern, your plan for ministry. Ideally, you won't need to take this book with you to the park. You may want to take a pen and paper to write down a person's name and number if they offer it to you.

Guidelines for Best Practice - Pray

- Pray before you go to the park. Pray that God will help you meet people who need to meet him. Pray that God would send you as a friend into their lives. Pray that God would cleanse your heart and life so you are ready to be his messenger.

- Pray while you're at the park. Pray for the people sitting around you by name (this will help you remember their names). Pray for God's blessing, guidance, and specifically for the salvation of the people around you. Pray for God to shape you into the friend these people need.

- Pray when you get home. Ask God to help you see or meet these same people again the next time you go back. Ask God to build a friendship with them so you can minister to them. Ask God to use you in their lives in the way they need it most.

Guidelines for Best Practice - Ask

- Sit in an area near people. Say hi when you sit down. "My name is ___." Usually people will tell you their name in response. Listen and remember their name. Write it down if you have to.

- If you are alone, try to connect with people of the same gender. This isn't a dating-plan; it's an outreach ministry.

- When you ask someone a question, be sure to ask them something that doesn't require them to risk anything if they choose to answer. Don't ask, "What's the worst thing you've ever done?" People won't tell you that until they trust you. Ask them something innocent, like...
    - Do you come to the park every week?
    - Do you know someone in the band?
    - What's your favorite kind of music?
    - How many kids to you have?
    - Where do you work?

- Look for ways to steer the conversation toward God, the Bible, church, heaven, prayer, etc. For example, if the weather is nice, you could say, "I thank God for such a beautiful day." Or if the music is nice, you could say, "I was praying for a relaxing weekend."
- IDEA - Buy some bubbles or a bubble gun. Blowing bubbles is an instant way to connect with kids. Their parents aren't far behind.

- IDEA - Bring a ball or frisbee. Be purposeful about inviting others to play with you. (You're at a park. It's okay to play).

Guidelines for Best Practice - Recruit

- Some people may have no interest in you or your God. Be sensitive. Pay attention to their reaction to you. Don't be pushy. If they don't want to talk to you, let them enjoy themselves and the music. If they don't want to talk about God, respect it and move on.

- If they seem friendly toward you, use this opportunity to gently invite them to worship. Think of how much you enjoy our church. They will too.

- It's helpful to have the address and times of worship already written down. Ask Pastor Steve for cards you can hand out.

- Limit yourself to one person or family per week. Don't be in a rush. And don't go from person to person repeating the same thing. People will see through this. Your goal is to build a genuine friendship that will lead to an opportunity to share Christ with them.

- If the person invites you to their church, mosque, synagogue, party, etc. try to go. This will show them that you are interested in the friendship, not just interested in making a "convert" to your church.

- If a person gives an excuse for not coming to worship as if they aren't good enough, you can gently remind them that "While we were still sinners, Christ died for us" (Romans 5:8) and Jesus came to save the lost, not to save people who don't need help (Luke 19:10).

- If they say no when you recruit them, that's okay. Don't feel defeated. Don't give up. I have invited dozens of people to worship (just in the last three months) and none have come (yet, my friend... yet).

- If they say no, still be friendly. You may be able to try again another time. Don't burn bridges.

Guidelines for Best Practice - Keep On

- Talk with other people who are participating in Purpose at the Park to share your ideas, concerns, and victories with each other. If you have a suggestion, share it with the group. If you have a question or concern, ask for help. Although you'll be ministering alone or with your spouse at the park, remember that there is a whole group of people who are doing the same thing.

- IDEA - Host a party for your neighbors or friends. Then invite your new friend from the park to come. Give the party a fun theme, like Mexican food and decor, bring a topping to build-your-own [fill in the blank... ice cream sundae, pizza, etc].

- IDEA - Have a game night. This works well, especially if your friend from the park has children. They can bring their favorite game or use yours.

- IDEA - Invite them to come early next week for a picnic with you before the music begins. Everyone brings their own food. Pick a location and time to meet.

- IDEA - Have a garage sale. Invite them to stop by. Or invite them to bring items to sell with you. This works especially well if you live near them.

Add your ideas here...

____

____

____

____

____

____

____

____

____

____

____

____

____

____

If a person asks you how to be saved...

Who knows? You might actually meet a person who is ready to receive salvation. We know that we cannot *earn* our way into heaven, that our sin earns death, and that eternal life is a gift from God that cannot be earned. Yet there are a few things God tells us to do in order to receive salvation. You'll want to be familiar with these four steps so you can talk about them if someone asks you.

- **God wants us to have faith** – Ephesians 2:8-10 is the clearest instruction for us to be saved by faith. More than belief (James 2:19), faith means putting our trust into action (James 2:17, 22). Also see Romans 10:9-10, Luke 8:12, and Mark 1:15.

- **God wants us to say it (to confess)** – Romans 10 says "If you declare with your mouth 'Jesus is Lord,' and believe in your heart that God raised him from the dead, you will be saved. For it is with your heart that you believe and are justified, and it is with your mouth that you profess your faith and are saved... everyone who call son the name of the Lord will be saved" (9-10, 13 NIV).

- **God wants us to turn away from sin (to repent).** He doesn't forgive us so we can keep on sinning. He forgives us and helps us to stop. Jesus said clearly that his purpose was to "call sinners to repentance" (Luke 5:32, 13:3-5). In Peter's great sermon in Acts

3, he instructs us to "Repent, then, and turn to God, so that your sins may be wiped out" (v 19).

- **God wants us to be baptized.** Baptism is a part of salvation. We are commanded to be baptized to be saved (Acts 2:37-38). In John 3:5, Jesus said, "I tell you the truth, no one can enter the kingdom of God unless he is born of water and the Spirit." Also see Mark 16:16.
    - Baptism isn't a bath for your body; it's a bath for your soul (1 Peter 3:21).
    - Baptism is an outward sign of the new life inside us (2 Corinthians 5:17).
    - Baptism connects the death (end) of our sin with Jesus' death and our new life with Jesus' resurrection (Romans 6:1-4)
    - Baptism show people a sign of our faith in Christ, as obviously seen as the clothes we wear (Galatians 3:27)

If they have additional questions, encourage them to read Galatians, a short book in the Bible that asks and answers many questions about salvation. Be sure to encourage them to come with you to worship. They'll want to meet your pastor, hear a sermon, and experience the loving family of your congregation.

Weekly Readings

Week 1 Today's date ____________

God's Word...

Jesus went through all the towns and villages, teaching in their synagogues, proclaiming the good news of the kingdom and healing every disease and sickness. When he saw the crowds, he had compassion on them, because they were harassed and helpless, like sheep without a shepherd. Then he said to his disciples, "The harvest is plentiful but the workers are few. Ask the Lord of the harvest, therefore, to send out workers into his harvest field."

~ Matthew 9:35-38 NIV

Thoughts to Ponder...

- Jesus didn't sit at home or stay inside a church building.
- Jesus looked at people through the lens of compassion.
- Few people are willing to do what Jesus did. Pray for them.

Action Steps...

- Memorize the words from the acronym for PARK (Pray, Ask, Recruit, and Keep On). This will be your basic pattern, your plan for ministry.
- Your goal is to connect with one person (or family).

- Pray silently for them. Think about them through the lens of compassion. Consider their needs. Ask God to help.
- Ask them something, anything, such as their name.
- If they seem friendly toward you, recruit them to worship. Say, “I belong to a great church. I think you should too. Would you like to come to worship with me on Sunday?”
- Choose an idea for how to Keep On. See the Best Practice section for ideas.

Week 2 **Today’s date ____________**

Reflect...

What worked well last week? What do you wish could have been better? What would need to change for this outreach plan to work?

God's Word...

For “Everyone who calls on the name of the Lord will be saved.” But how can they call on him to save them unless they believe in him? And how can they believe in him if they have never heard about him? And how can they hear about him unless someone tells them? And how will anyone go and tell them without being sent? That is why the

Scriptures say, “How beautiful are the feet of messengers who bring good news!”

~ Romans 10:13-15 NLT

Thoughts to Ponder...

- Jesus sent us to share the good news about him
- The Bible says when we do this, we are beautiful
- If we don’t do it, some people may never know

Action Steps...

- Your goal is to reconnect with the person or family you met last week. If you can’t do this within the first half-hour, try to connect with another person or family.
- Pray for the person you met last week and the person you’ll meet today. Pray for their salvation.
- Ask them something. If this is your second conversation, build from the last time you talked. Let the conversation grow naturally.
- If they seem friendly toward you, recruit them to worship. Say, “We have a special worship service planned at our church this Sunday. I think you might like to come.” Let them respond.
- Choose another idea from the Best Practice section about how to Keep On.

Week 3 **Today's date** ____________

Reflect...

Did it feel "beautiful" last week to build a purposeful friendship with someone who needs Jesus? What worked well last week? What do you wish could have been better? What would need to change for this outreach plan to work?

God's Word...

The Lord gave me a message. He said, "Son of man, I have appointed you as a watchman for Israel. Whenever you receive a message from me, warn people immediately. If I warn the wicked, saying, 'You are under the penalty of death,' but you fail to deliver the warning, they will die in their sins. And I will hold you responsible for their deaths. If you warn them and they refuse to repent and keep on sinning, they will die in their sins. But you will have saved yourself because you obeyed me.

~ Ezekiel 3:16-19 NLT

Thoughts to Ponder...

- The Lord asked Ezekiel to be responsible for the people around him. What responsibility do we have?
- What is the natural consequence of sin? What is the spiritual consequence?
- What happens to people who never escape the consequences of their sin?

Action Steps…

- If this is your third meeting with the same person or family, it might be a good time to trade phone numbers.
- Your goal is to reconnect with the same people. If you can't do this within the first half-hour, try to connect with another person or family.
- Pray for the people you've met and the person you'll meet today. Pray for their salvation.
- Ask them something. Build the conversation from the last time you talked.
- If they seem friendly toward you, recruit them to worship. Say, "We have a special worship service planned at our church this Sunday. I think you might like to come." Let them respond.
- Choose another idea from the Best Practice section about how to Keep On.

Week 4 **Today's date ______________**

Reflect…

Like Ezekiel, have you taken responsibility for the people around you? What worked well last week? What do you wish could have been better? What would need to change for this outreach plan to work?

God's Word...

In the beginning the Word already existed. He was with God, and he was God. So the Word became human and lived here on earth among us. He was full of unfailing love and faithfulness. And we have seen his glory, the glory of the only Son of the Father.

~ John 1:1 & 14 NLT

Thoughts to Ponder...

- Jesus, the "Word," didn't stay in heaven; he came with live with us. Where have you been living, spending most of your time?
- When Jesus moved in, he brought unfailing love and faithfulness with him. What are you bringing?
- When people looked at Jesus, they saw God. What do people see when they look at you?

Action Steps...

- Your goal is to reconnect with the same people. If you can't do this within the first half-hour, try to connect with another person or family.
- Pray for the people you've met and the person you'll meet today. Pray for their salvation.
- Ask them something. Build the conversation from the last time you talked.
- If they seem friendly toward you, recruit them to worship. Say, "We have a special worship service planned at our church this Sunday. I think you might like to come." Let them respond.
- Choose another idea from the Best Practice section about how to Keep On.

Week 5 **Today's date _____________**

Reflect...

Does your routine keep you from interacting with people who need Jesus? Can others see evidence of Jesus in your life? What worked well last week? What do you wish could have been better? What would need to change for this outreach plan to work?

God's Word...

The seed that fell on the hard path represents those who hear the Good News about the Kingdom and don't understand it. Then the evil one comes and snatches the seed away from their hearts.

The rocky soil represents those who hear the message and receive it with joy. But like young plants in such soil, their roots don't go very deep. At first they get along fine, but they wilt as soon as they have problems or are persecuted because they believe the word.

The thorny ground represents those who hear and accept the Good News, but all too quickly the message is crowded out by the cares of this life and the lure of wealth, so no crop is produced.

The good soil represents the hearts of those who truly accept God's message and produce a huge harvest – thirty, sixty, or even a hundred times as much as had been planted.

~ Matthew 13:19-23 NLT

Thoughts to Ponder...

- In this parable, only one out of four seeds grew into a healthy plant. Why?
- Inviting people into our Christian community is a great way to help their roots “go deep.” How else does this happen?
- When we help with the “cares of this life” for people, they are more ready to hear the Good News about Jesus. What can you do to provide in a practical way for others’ needs?

Action Steps...

- Hopefully by now you’ve begun to build a friendship. Be sure to take specific steps to Keep On moving forward in this new relationship.
- Your goal is to reconnect with the same people. If you can’t do this within the first half-hour, try to connect with another person or family.
- Pray for the people you’ve met and the person you’ll meet today. Pray for their salvation.
- Ask them something. Build the conversation from the last time you talked.
- If they seem friendly toward you, recruit them to worship. Say, “We have a special worship service planned at our church this Sunday. I think you might like to come.” Let them respond.

Week 6 **Today's date ____________**

Reflect…

As you have been meeting people at the park, what kind of "soil" would you used to describe them (hard path, rocky path, thorny ground, or good soil)? What worked well last week? What do you wish could have been better? What would need to change for this outreach plan to work?

God's Word…

Philip ran over and heard the man reading from the prophet Isaiah. Philip asked, "Do you understand what you are reading?" The man replied, "How can I, unless someone instructs me?" And he urged Philip to come up into the carriage and sit with him.

~ Acts 8:30-31 NLT

Thoughts to Ponder…

- Like this person, people are often curious about God, but not sure how to learn more.
- Philip made himself available to answer this person's questions about Jesus. How are you making yourself available?
- Philip's readiness led to this person's salvation. How have you specifically made yourself ready?

Action Steps...

- If you haven't already, read the section at the beginning of this book about your answer if a person asks you how to be saved.
- Your goal is to reconnect with the same people. If you can't do this within the first half-hour, try to connect with another person or family.
- Pray for the people you've met and the person you'll meet today. Pray for their salvation.
- Ask them something. Build the conversation from the last time you talked.
- If they seem friendly toward you, recruit them to worship. Say, "We have a special worship service planned at our church this Sunday. I think you might like to come." Let them respond.
- Choose another idea from the Best Practice section about how to Keep On.

Week 7 **Today's date** ______________

Reflect...

Like Philip, have you listened and obeyed the Lord's direction to speak with others about Jesus? What worked well last week? What do you wish could have been better? What would need to change for this outreach plan to work?

God's Word...

Now, who will want to harm you if you are eager to do good? But even if you suffer for doing what is right, God will reward you for it. So don't be afraid and don't worry. Instead, you must worship Christ as Lord of your life. And if someone asks about your Christian hope, always be ready to explain it. But do this in a gentle and respectful way.

~ 1 Peter 3:13-16 NLT

Thoughts to Ponder...

- What is the worst thing you could "suffer" if you share the Good News of Jesus with someone?
- What does it mean for Jesus Christ to be the "Lord of your life?"
- How can you be ready to gently and respectfully explain your hope in Christ?

Action Steps...

- Your goal is to reconnect with the same people. If you can't do this within the first half-hour, try to connect with another person or family.
- Pray for the people you've met and the person you'll meet today. Pray for their salvation.
- Ask them something. Build the conversation from the last time you talked.
- If they seem friendly toward you, recruit them to worship. Say, "We have a special worship service planned at our church this Sunday. I think you might like to come." Let them respond.
- Choose another idea from the Best Practice section about how to Keep On.

Week 8 **Today's date ____________**

Reflect...

What should you do if someone asks you a question about Jesus that you aren't sure how to answer? What worked well last week? What do you wish could have been better? What would need to change for this outreach plan to work?

God's Word...

Then the Lord told Abram, "Leave your country, your relatives, and your father's house, and go to the land that I will show you. I will cause you to become the father of a great nation. I will bless you and make you famous, and I will make you a blessing to others. I will bless those who bless you and curse those who curse you. All the families of the earth will be blessed through you."

~ Genesis 12:1-4 NLT

Thoughts to Ponder...

- God gave many blessing to Abraham. Who were these blessings for, him or others?
- How has God blessed you?
- How can you use these blessings to bless other people?

Action Steps...

- Your goal is to reconnect with the same people. If you can't do this within the first half-hour, try to connect with another person or family.
- Pray for the people you've met and the person you'll meet today. Pray for their salvation.
- Ask them something. Build the conversation from the last time you talked.
- If they seem friendly toward you, recruit them to worship. Say, "We have a special worship service planned at our church this Sunday. I think you might like to come." Let them respond.
- Choose another idea from the Best Practice section about how to Keep On.

Additional Reading

To continue your learning and experience in outreach ministry, here are some additional Scriptures you'll want to study.

[___] Luke 19:10 - Why did Jesus come?

[___] Acts 1:8 - Where does the strength we need to be a witness for Jesus come from?

[___] Matthew 28:18-20 - What did Jesus send us to do?

[___] John 14:6 - How can people get into heaven?

[___] Isaiah 6:8 - When the Lord asks for someone to be his messenger, will you answer the way Isaiah did?

[___] Psalm 19:1-6 - Can you see God at work in his creation? What does it tell you about him?

[___] Matthew 13:3-8, 18-23 - Think about when someone planted the "seed" of the Good News in you. What kind of soil were you at various times?

[___] Acts 8:26-38 - What did Philip do right? How can you follow his example?

[___] Romans 1:16 - Do you feel embarrassed or scared to talk with others about the Good News of Jesus?

How To Order This Book

For more information about buying copies of this book and others like it, please visit

http :// shop . my own little reality . com

(no spaces)

www.ingramcontent.com/pod-product-compliance
Ingram Content Group UK Ltd.
Pitfield, Milton Keynes, MK11 3LW, UK
UKHW020227250726
13967UKWH00001B/233